Original title:
Shadows in Snowfall

Copyright © 2024 Creative Arts Management OÜ
All rights reserved.

Author: Miriam Kensington
ISBN HARDBACK: 978-9916-94-530-8
ISBN PAPERBACK: 978-9916-94-531-5

The Silent Dance of Snow

The flakes flutter down with a flip,
As kids try to catch them on their lip.
With snowmen that wobble, topple, and spin,
They giggle and shout, let the fun begin!

Snowball fights break out with a cheer,
Dodging the blasts, nothing to fear.
Frosty noses and mittens all soaked,
With laughter and joy, it's all a joke!

Celestial Traces on the Ground

Stars have fallen from the sky,
Landing softly, oh my my!
They leave trails of laughter wide,
Dancing in the snow, they slide.

With footprints big and small in tow,
Chasing after each bright glow.
Oh, look! A comet made of ice,
Did it just wink? Ah, ain't that nice!

Lurking Figures in the Cold

Figures creep as snowflakes fall,
Is it a ghost? No, just a ball!
A snowman peeks from behind a tree,
With carrot nose, snickering with glee.

Snowy shapes sneak in the night,
Playing games in frosty light.
A funny hat, a scarf that sways,
It's colder here in comical ways!

Glistening Haze of the Dark

The moon is giggling, shining bright,
As it paints the world in soft white light.
Mischief lurks in every drift,
A frosty laugh is winter's gift.

Each slippery slope calls for a dash,
Down we go with a screeching crash!
With cheeks like roses and grins so wide,
Winter's charm is a joyride.

Glacial Dreams in Starlit Quiet

In the night, a penguin slides,
Dancing down where ice resides.
Snowflakes laugh, they prance and twirl,
As frosty whispers gently swirl.

A snowman with a carrot nose,
Tries to breakdance but just dozes.
His hat jumps up, his scarf's a mess,
He dreams of warmth, oh what excess!

Frozen frogs with winter flair,
Croak a tune, without a care.
Skiing squirrels in tiny boots,
Chasing flakes, those wiggly roots.

In glistening fields, clumsy deer,
Trip on snowballs, never fear.
They chuckle loud, a frosty cheer,
For laughter echoes, crystal-clear.

Remnants of Stillness Underneath

Beneath the white, a crab does waltz,
In flippers lost, he proudly exalts.
He spins and flips, with style and grace,
A frozen ballet, a quirky race.

The ice is slick, the rabbits slip,
Taking turns on the snowy trip.
They squeak and hop, and giggle with glee,
For winter chaos brings pure esprit.

A fox donning a fuzzy hat,
Attempts to catch a snowball bat.
Misses each time with style unbraced,
Yet finds his charm in every face.

Up above, a flock of geese,
Are plotting gigs for winter's lease.
They waddle down, embrace the fun,
In every nibble, laughs begun.

The Numbness of Forgotten Lore

Once a tale of a bunny bold,
Who wore a cape of shimmering gold.
He hopped through flakes without a fright,
Though fashionably odd, he felt just right.

A bear with goggles, lost his way,
Skis behind, in a snowy ballet.
He tumbles down with rounds of glee,
While singing songs of mishaps free.

The trees might whisper secrets lost,
Of frosty fights and winter's cost.
They giggle low with flurries bright,
In silence, echoes of pure delight.

In cozy nooks, where laughter sprawls,
Misfit creatures share funny calls.
For every story tucked away,
Brings warmth to chilly winter play.

Whirling Darkness in a White World

A raccoon with a dazzling hat,
Digs in snow like a royal brat.
He stumbles hard, then throws a laugh,
In his cool style, a winter gaffe.

A herd of moose, with scarves so loud,
Strut like kings, oh so proud.
They trip and tease, in frosty flair,
While snowflakes boogie in the air.

A snowball fight, the owls take aim,
Feathers fly in a frozen game.
They hoot and swoop, the fun they share,
In frosty duels, we shed every care.

So here we are, in winter's hold,
Finding joy in the bright and cold.
With laughter swirling through the night,
In every flake, a spark of light.

Whispers Beneath the White Veil

As flakes drift down with grace so light,
A snowman laughs, his eyes so bright.
He tells a joke, it's quite the sight,
But frozen puns? They don't ignite.

The trees wear coats of glistening white,
While squirrels scamper, a comical flight.
They slip and slide, oh what a fright,
But winter's giggles keep spirits bright.

Echoes on Frosted Paths

Footprints dance in a silly line,
Two dogs collide, oh how they whine!
A snowball flies, it's all benign,
But misses its mark, causing decline.

A couple strolls, their breath a plume,
Laughing as flakes create a doom.
With every slip, there's room for gloom,
Yet giggles rise, dispelling gloom.

Chasing Silhouettes in the Flurries

A cat leaps high, chasing the breeze,
But lands in snow with grace to tease.
Its whiskers frost, it's sure to freeze,
Yet purring loud, it seeks to please.

Kids tumble down like bags of fluff,
While frost bites cheeks, it's never tough.
They build a fort with all their stuff,
And giggle loud, their joy is rough.

Ghosts of Winter's Embrace

The moon looks down on scenes absurd,
As snowflakes twirl without a word.
A snow angel flaps, wings gently stirred,
With laughter ringing, feelings stirred.

A grumpy elf slips on the ground,
His candy cane sticks, he spins around.
With every fall, there's joy found,
For winter's humor knows no bound.

Ethereal Figures in the Snow

In winter's chill, a dance unfolds,
With snowflakes swirling, tales retold.
A snowman wobbles, a hat askew,
As penguins slide, who knew they flew?

Laughter echoes through icy air,
While rabbits hop without a care.
Yet, something lurks, a playful tease,
It's just a squirrel, please don't freeze!

Beyond The Veil of Flurries

A snowflake lands upon my nose,
And sneezes come, in winter's prose.
An icicle dangles, sharp and tall,
Like nature's sword, a cautious call.

Meanwhile, reindeer prance and play,
With clumsy leaps, they steal the day.
But just like us, they trip and fall,
A frosty dance, a winter ball!

Whispers of the Winter Night

In the stillness of a moonlit glow,
Whispers chase the flakes, soft and slow.
A cat in boots wanders outside,
Chasing shadows, oh what a ride!

A snowball fight breaks the calm delight,
With laughter ringing through the night.
But wait! Was that a ghostly sigh?
Just a snowman, too shy to lie!

Phantom Silhouettes in the Frost

Figures loom in dim moonlight,
Mischief making, oh what a sight!
A snow angel giggles, spreading wide,
While a dog in snow can't decide!

With frosty breath, the breeze does play,
It tickles noses, on winter's way.
Yet, beneath the stars so bright,
A bogeyman snores, what a fright!

Secrets in the Snowbound Silence

The snowflakes dance, a silly sight,
As snowmen giggle in pure delight.
A penguin slips, does a funny spin,
While rabbits plot their next big win.

But watch out for the snowball fights,
As reindeer laugh in cozy nights.
The winter air, so crisp and clear,
Brings out our jokes, oh what a cheer!

With hot cocoa in hand we scheme,
A winter's joke is quite the dream.
We hide behind a frosty tree,
And throw surprise, oh look at me!

In whispers soft, we share our plans,
For snowball battles and snowflake dance.
The snowbound silence fills with glee,
As laughter echoes, wild and free.

Hazy Dreams in the Winter's Grasp

The winter air gives quite the chill,
As squirrels scurry, oh what a thrill!
A fog of dreams, where snowflakes twist,
And all our worries, we dare to miss.

In fuzzy hats and mismatched gloves,
We make our moves and share our loves.
A snowman's nose, a carrot bright,
With candy eyes, what a silly sight!

We take a tumble, in frosty fun,
Rolling and laughing, oh how we run!
In fluffy coats, we chase our dreams,
While winter whispers in silvery beams.

So let's build forts and watch them fall,
With giggles echoing, we'll have a ball.
The haze of winter wraps us tight,
In dreams of laughter, pure delight.

Vespertine Whispers on Frost

As evening falls with a twinkling sky,
We dance in laughter, spirits high.
The snowflakes giggle, the moon winks too,
Creating a scene quite merry and new.

In warm mittens, we plot and plan,
With frosty fun, we take a stand.
A snowball flies, laughter ensues,
As friends collide in playful ruse.

With the spark of dusk, our spirits lift,
In snowy fields, we find our gift.
The whispers beckon us to play,
In winter's chill, we seize the day.

So gather round, my frosty friends,
For vespertine fun, the laughter never ends.
With twirls and leaps, we spin with ease,
In chilly air, we find our freeze.

Glimmers of Light on Dusk's Canvas

When winter comes to play with snow,
The moon slips in, a cheeky glow.
Snowmen dance, all plump and round,
While squirrels slide without a sound.

With snowflakes falling, giggles rise,
Frosty hats, they wear as guise.
A penguin waltz upon the street,
A furry slip, oh, what a feat!

Snowballs fly like crafty darts,
Bouncing off the icy hearts.
Giggles echo through the night,
As laughter shimmers, pure delight.

Embrace the chill with silly cheer,
For winter's magic brings us near.
In the fluff, our joys compile,
Who knew snow could bring such style?

Enigmatic Shapes Beneath the Drift

Beneath the fluff, a lump so strange,
A snowman's nose, a funny range.
Did he borrow that from a tree?
Or is it just a mystery?

Rabbits hop with a thumping beat,
While snowflakes land on furry feet.
A poodle prances in the white,
Doing twirls with sheer delight.

The flakes conspire, swirl and dance,
Whisper tales of odd romance.
A snowball fight, the game is on,
Laughter bursts until it's gone.

So join the fun, no need to fret,
In winter's arms, we won't forget.
Each shape that forms invites a grin,
As chilly winds join in the din.

Moonlit Hues on Winter's Canvas

Under the stars, the shadows prance,
With moonlit beams, they start to dance.
Sledging down a snowy hill,
The laughter echoes, what a thrill!

Hot cocoa brews with marshmallow cheer,
While snowflakes twirl, oh-so-dear.
A snowball rolls, the dog takes chase,
As everyone joins in the race.

Giggling kids with cheeks aglow,
Sprinkling joy with every throw.
The night wears white, a frosty gown,
Creativity's never brown!

Let's carve our dreams in sparkling frost,
Adventures made, no moment lost.
With every drift, a smile we spin,
In this fun, we all can win!

Veils of Ice and Memory

In ethereal drifts, we play,
Where winter's quirk brings joy each day.
Frosty breath, like dragons' puffs,
While the world wraps in winter's cuffs.

Pine trees wear their coats of white,
As snowflakes twinkle, oh-so-bright.
A yule log rolls, it's time to cheer,
Awaiting 'Santa' to appear!

With each crunch on the icy ground,
Another laughter, or so it's found.
The mysteries hide in frosty grace,
As we forge joy in every place.

Let mischievous spirits take the lead,
As we dance in snow, a playful deed.
In memory's grasp, we twirl and glide,
With winter wonder, we take pride.

Whispering Secrets Beneath Ice Tapestry

Snowmen gossip beneath frosty trees,
While falling flakes tease with a playful breeze.
A rabbit rushes, dressed in winter wear,
Searching for carrots in the icy air.

Penguins slide past, with comical grace,
Waddling along in a snowball race.
Hot cocoa spills, a frothy delight,
As snowflakes giggle in the pale moonlight.

A snowball fight breaks, laughter ignites,
With poofy hats bobbing into wild frights.
But as they tumble, roll, and spin,
Snow angels await, let the fun begin!

Winter's Unseen Masks in the Glow

Frozen faces peek around the bend,
Mittens waving, rivalries they pretend.
A puppy frolics, lost in white fluff,
Chasing its tail, oh, winter is tough!

Glistening icicles hang like odd hair,
Silly snowflakes land on noses bare.
With every slip and tumble we see,
Laughter echoes, as bright as can be.

The jingle of sleds confirms the spree,
While snow-wipe faces laugh merrily.
Hats on the ground, and scarves in a mess,
Oh, the hilarity of winter's duress!

The Flicker of Time in Snow's Grasp

Time takes a break, as snowflakes parade,
Each one a dancer in a delicate charade.
Children giggle, donning gear piled high,
As great-grandma's recipe floats by!

A snow fort rises, with bright flags that sway,
As ninja squirrels plot their heist on display.
A flurry of laughter, sleds fast in flight,
Whipping round corners, oh what a sight!

But lo! A misstep, and down they go,
Rolling in snow like a live comedy show.
So grab your mittens, come join in the fun,
For winter's a circus, and we're all the clowns!

Ethereal Hues Where Snowflakes Dawdle

Sparkling white swirls where giggles erupt,
A world wrapped in magic, so brilliantly cupped.
Snowflakes jive, swaying under the sun,
Creating a spectacle, the best kind of fun!

Chubby penguins with waddles en vogue,
Dance with the trees, giving the cold a rogue.
A lost mitten found, cuddly above,
As winter reveals its hidden love!

With every snowball, a story is brewed,
Of laughter and mishaps, a joyous mood.
So let's raise a glass of snow-laden cheer,
In this whimsical land, we have nothing to fear!

Ghostly Visions on Winter's Breath

Flakes dance and twirl in the air,
While snowmen plot with a frosty stare.
One whispers, 'Hey, I lost my nose!'
The carrot thief giggles, then it froze.

Frosty friends all slip and slide,
Wobbling like penguins, filled with pride.
They gather round for a snowball fight,
But end up buried, oh what a sight!

A ghostly laugh floats through the night,
With every puff, they take their flight.
One ghostly friend tries to make a splash,
But lands headfirst in the icy mash.

So as they bumble while trying to play,
Each frosty spirit shouts out, "Yay!"
In the goofy glow of winter's glow,
They dance among the flakes—D'oh, oh no!

Nightfall's Crystalline Charades

Underneath the twinkling glow,
The frostbitten giggles begin to flow.
Candles flicker, a bunny hops,
Wearing mittens, it's all that stops.

A snowflake falls right on a nose,
With a sneeze so loud, the laughter grows.
Snowball dodging leads to a slip,
As friends topple down, a frosty trip.

A winter cat in a fuzzy hat,
Hypnotizes snowmen, fancy that!
They jive and twist like glamorous stars,
Bumping off each other—Look out! Puddles of cars!

Whispers of giggling through the cold,
Warmest stories of winter told.
Under the lights, they laugh come what may,
For a night of fun, wrapped in a snowy ballet.

Secrets Cradled in Snow's Embrace

With each droplet of snow that lands,
The world becomes a playground made of bands.
Snowmen gossip about winter flaws,
Whispering tales 'neath furry paws.

The reindeer prance with little grace,
Trying hard not to lose their face.
They juggle snowballs, a snowy show,
Until they slip and fly to and fro.

Under the moon, peculiar sounds rise,
Hoots and laughs fill the starry skies.
A goofy raccoon in a knitted scarf,
Sings silly tunes creating a laugh.

When morning comes in a blanket of white,
They cuddle close, what a funny sight!
Memories cached in snow's soft bed,
Every chuckle warming hearts instead.

Wisps of White Through the Gloom

Fluffy clouds drift with playful grins,
As silly games begin where fun begins.
Snowflakes pop like confetti in cheer,
Each one carries a giggle so near.

In a playful race, the children zoom,
Hot cocoa tumbling, despite the gloom.
They build a fort, make snow-angel friends,
Until someone shouts, "This never ends!"

A snowflakes' ballet, quite a charade,
As wacky moves create a parade.
Elves with bells dance atop the snow,
Leaps and twists, stealing the show!

So when winter bids us goodnight,
And the moon glimmers with a tiny light,
We'll carry the laughter, the warm memory,
That joy can snowball in every glee.

Dances of Dusk on Winter's Canvas

Beneath the silvery glow,
Socks slide on icy floors,
With giggles and wild throws,
We tumble through snowy doors.

A snowball fight erupts,
Laughter echoes and bounces,
While frosty flakes disrupt,
All our careful prounces.

We twirl like winter's best,
In a merry, frosty spree,
Each spin puts us to test,
Fueling our circus glee.

As night wraps the land tight,
Light-hearted chaos reigns,
In this chilly delight,
Fun hooks with no refrains.

Veiled Figures in a Crystal Dream

Wearing coats three sizes too big,
We waddle like penguins bold,
Falling flat on our own gig,
In laughter, warmth unfolds.

A snowman sports a bright hat,
With carrot nose askew,
He surely looks a bit fat,
But he's jolly, it's true!

We chase our dreams in the cold,
With snowflakes in our hair,
In antics, we're bright and bold,
Creating memories rare.

As moonlight brushes the ground,
The air sparkles with fun,
With each cheerful sound,
Our playful hearts have won.

Frosted Phantoms at Twilight

The wind whispers silly tales,
Of reindeer in disguise,
As we dodge those icy gales,
And dance beneath the skies.

A frosty breath of giggles,
Puffs into misty air,
We scatter like little wiggles,
Chasing snowflakes in the flare.

Costume party out in snow,
As reindeer, we prance wide,
Under stars that promise glow,
We forget our winter pride.

With cheeks rosy and bright,
We twirl through the cold's embrace,
Our laughter's pure delight,
Leaves footprints in our chase.

Footprints in the Unseen

We tread on the sparkling ground,
With squeaky boots in line,
Following sound all around,
To find where we can dine.

The ice makes us slip and slide,
As our hot cocoa spills,
But silliness is our guide,
Through winter's funny drills.

Oh, to be a snowball's flight,
Dodging kids with a laugh,
In this chill, pure delight,
We embrace winter's gaffe.

With each frolic, we create,
A trail of giggles bright,
In each wild move, we celebrate,
The magic of winter's night.

The Secret Life of Silent Drifts

Behind the white, the whispers play,
A snowman doing the cha-cha sway.
Icicles giggle as they hang,
While little birds rush by, all sang.

Bunnies in boots, who'd think it so?
Sledding on planks, oh what a show!
Frosty felines trying to pounce,
On snowflakes dancing, they all bounce.

Winter's here and mischief runs,
The snowflakes chuckle, just for fun.
Peppermint sticks looking so sly,
As candy canes leap, oh my, oh my!

Snowballs tossed with cheeky delight,
Snow angels plotting in the night.
Behind the drifts, giggling ensues,
As laughter floats on frosty views.

Transient Forms in Icy Light

In frozen frames, the hoot owls laugh,
As penguins in ties write a silly chaff.
Flakes twirl around in a dizzy display,
While squirrels in hats start the frosty ballet.

The winter dog prancing like a star,
Chasing his tail near the snowman bazaar.
Fuzzy gloves wave like they're in a dance,
While mittens conspire in a winter romance.

Snow drifts and giggles, a playful affair,
Frost bit toes, but no one would care.
With snowmen debating who's the best,
They giggle and wiggle, never at rest.

In twinkling nights, with lanterns aglow,
They share their stories, as soft breezes flow.
With feet in the frost, laughter is found,
In shapes of the night, joy goes around.

Murmurs of the Snowbound Night

The moon plays tricks on powdery white,
As critters have fun in the frosty night.
Snowflakes waltz in their chilly ball,
While tinsel bats giggle, flipping tall.

Under cold stars, the grumpy old cat,
Tries to chase snowflakes that dance on his hat.
With snowball fights causing a ruckus near,
The snowman melts with laughter and cheer.

In crowded drifts, the gossip takes flight,
A whisper of snowmen in the moonlight.
Chunks of ice with a comedic flair,
They tumble and roll without a care.

Nighttime frolics with giggles and grins,
While chilly skaters tussle for wins.
The secrets of snow in the stillness hum,
As they dream up more, oh such winter fun!

Enigmas Wrapped in Winter's Cloak

Wrapped in ice, the secrets stay,
While snowflakes plot their mischievous play.
Chimney sweeps in folly and jest,
As marshmallows roast, they're quite the guest.

The snowman declares himself the king,
As penguins march and the winterbirds sing.
Guffaws erupt from valleys and hills,
When a big snowball causes winter spills.

With laughter that echoes through frosty trees,
Hot cocoa swirls with giggles and tease.
The puzzles of ice tickle the ground,
As frosty friends gather 'round and around.

Tootsie-pollies in the chilly air,
They dance on rooftops without a care.
In the secretive still, the fun won't cease,
As winter's riddles bring all to peace.

Ethereal Echoes in the Silent Storm

A snowman dreams of a sunlit day,
With carrot nose, he'll melt away.
He hopes for warmth, a gentle breeze,
But here he stands, with frozen knees.

The snowflakes laugh as they tumble down,
Tickling noses of every clown.
They swirl and swirl, like they know a joke,
As frosty air makes us all choke.

Chasing snowflakes, we trip and fall,
With rosy cheeks, we can't recall.
The cheerful shouts, the slippery slide,
In winter's grip, we take the ride.

But giggles rise amidst the chill,
As snowballs fly with perfect skill.
We join the fun, through drifts we dash,
Creating memories in a winter's splash.

The Dance of Light and Cold

Frosty friends in a winter waltz,
They twirl and glide without a fault.
But one too fast, he takes a dive,
And lands with grace - who needs to thrive?

Snowflakes prance like little sprites,
Pirouetting under moonlit nights.
With laughter ringing through the trees,
They plot and scheme with frosty tease.

Cold noses meet with warm delights,
As cocoa spills in snowy fights.
Snow forts rise, laughter in the air,
In this chilled dance, no need to fear.

But careful now, the ground is slick,
Watch for the ice or take a trick.
In layers thick, we tumble and roll,
Making silly memories, heart and soul.

Silken Threads of the Frigid Air

A squirrel in winter's finest coat,
Chases his tail on a frosted moat.
With acorns stored, he leaps with glee,
As icicles dangle, tempting spree.

Puffy coats, we waddle like ducks,
While laughter rings, we're out of luck.
With snowball fights and frosty cheers,
We stumble through these joyful years.

But sledding down the hill so steep,
We giggle loud, and then we leap.
Landslide of snow, a giant puff,
That's just how we like our luck!

With every tumble, and every laugh,
The winter's scene becomes our craft.
In icy bliss, warmth is found,
A funny chill that knows no bounds.

Secrets Lost in the Bitter Chill

The wind whispers tales of the past,
As ice turns rivers into cast.
Snowy blankets hide each nook,
With secret giggles, our hearts took.

Elf hats bob on heads like grapes,
Through frosted fields, we make our shapes.
Each frosty breath, a puff of fun,
As winter's magic's softly spun.

The snowdrifts fold like fleeting dreams,
In every step, the laughter seems.
As we splash in puddles dressed in white,
With silly antics, all feels right.

But springs will catch us unaware,
With melted joys and warm sun's glare.
Until next winter, we'll smile and play,
For fun never left, it's here to stay.

Hushed Footprints on White

Tiny prints upon the ground,
A raccoon's dance, oh what a sound!
With every step, they wiggle and sway,
As if they've lost their way today.

A cat walks by, all proud and slick,
Then slips and rolls—oh, that was quick!
The snowflakes laugh, they shimmy and glide,
While every creature takes a wild ride.

A squirrel pops in, all fluffy and round,
Sliding down hills, making no sound.
With acorn in tow, he tries to leap,
But tumbles through powder—oh, what a heap!

Bunnies prance without a care,
Turning white fluff into a fair.
Look at them go with their boundless cheer,
Winter's comic show, the best time of year!

Silhouettes Amidst Snowflakes

Hats flying off in the winter breeze,
A snowman's grin, that's sure to please.
But then, oh no! His hat takes flight,
A chase ensues, such a silly sight!

Birds in winter, they dance and dive,
In the thick white air, they seem so alive.
One lands on a branch, and it's quite the scene,
For he's got a dash of bright red sheen.

Furry creatures hop and skip,
With tails a-wagging, they take a dip.
In piles of snow, they roll and flop,
Sharing giggles, they just can't stop!

Children build castles, they aim and throw,
But hit each other with two feet of snow.
Laughter erupts with a joyful cheer,
As winter's playtime brings everyone near!

Chilling Ghosts of Winter

A frosty breeze gives me a shiver,
Is that a ghost, or just a river?
With sheets of white that flow and sway,
I'm convinced I've got ghosts at play!

A chilly specter with snow-white mitt,
Lost in laughter, he just won't quit.
He tips his hat, gives me a wink,
Then disappears with nary a blink!

Sleigh bells jingle with a ghostly name,
Hitching a ride—it's all a game!
Yet somehow they leave no sleigh tracks,
Just giggles echoing through the cracks.

Through piles of snow, they glide with glee,
With a flip and a swirl, they tickle me.
What fun it is to share their night,
With frosty haunts and laughter's delight!

Flickering Forms in the Frost

In the chilly night, what a sight to see,
A dance of light, oh wait, is that me?
With every twirl, my feet get too bold,
And down I go, just like it's been told!

Frosty silhouettes play peek-a-boo,
I swear one winked, and then it flew!
Silly forms in a magical glow,
Mimic my fall, oh how they flow!

The trees wear coats of sparkling frost,
While snowflakes swirl, who cares who's lost?
I splat face-first, yet burst into giggles,
As that frozen galoot does the wiggly wiggles!

Each flickering shape inside the chill,
Offers a chuckle, it's such a thrill.
In this winter's tale of playful tease,
We dance and tumble with the greatest ease!

Veils of Gray on a White Terrain

Snowflakes fall, a frosty dance,
Hats askew with a giggling glance.
Penguins slide, their bellies so round,
If only they'd learned, they'd not hit the ground.

A snowman built with a carrot nose,
Now sporting a hat that nobody chose.
In this winter's embrace, we find delight,
As laughing squirrels make off in flight.

Elves try to ski, oh what a sight,
Tangled in snow, they vanish from light.
Snowball fights rage, but all in good fun,
As laughter erupts in the crisp winter sun.

The crunching of snow 'neath comic delight,
Footprints lead to mischief, oh what a night!
Whimsy afloat in the icy cheer,
Who knew winter could bring such a leer!

Figures in the Hush of December

In the stillness of cold, we hear a cheer,
A snowflake's chuckle as it lands near.
Chubby cheeks and noses aglow,
They frolic around, putting on a show.

A group of friends, wrapped up tight,
Laughing loudly, their joy takes flight.
Making shapes in the snow, oh how they pose,
The 'masterpiece' shows all their toes!

Mittens mispaired and boots covered in fluff,
Sleds flip over, the fun's never enough.
With twirls and spins, they play, merry and wild,
It's hard to tell now who's the grown child.

Hot cocoa awaits with marshmallows stacked,
But first, a snowball fight, it's all intact.
Giggles echo in the frosty scene,
In December's hush, they're all so keen!

Fading Imprints Beneath the Flakes

Imprints in white where the mischief lies,
Little feet dance, with playful surprise.
A puppy plunges, he's bound to fall,
Leaving a paw print for us all.

Sliding down hills, oh what a blast,
Watch your speed or you'll tumble fast!
Laughter erupts as a friend does a flip,
Lands with a thud, what a humorous trip!

Snowballs are flying, a fluffy brigade,
The art of the throw, an ambitious charade.
Faces all gleam with mischievous glee,
"Did you get me or was it the tree?"

As daylight fades and the frost settles in,
Each giggle immortal, the joy can't wear thin.
From fading imprints, memories will sprout,
Winter's a chuckle, beyond any doubt!

Illusions in the Winter's Breath

Chill in the air, the trees wear white,
They whisper stories, tales in the night.
The snow's a blanket, thick on the ground,
While squirrels wiggle and spin 'round and 'round.

The frost means business, or so it seems,
But ice cubes slide in my warm cocoa dreams.
Fluffy snowflakes tumble and engage,
Is that a snow ghoul? Turns out a sage!

Laughter erupts as kids try to catch,
A misguided snowball's a slippery batch.
With each chilly gust and gusty cheer,
Winter's a jester, come join in the flair.

Mirages of warmth in this frosty place,
Cold as a winter but full of grace.
Illusions of fun amid flakes all aglow,
Who knew that winter could steal the show?

Ephemeral Ghosts of Winter Woods

In frosty woods, a laugh takes flight,
Snowflakes giggle in the pale moonlight.
The branches sway with a playful cheer,
Winter's jesters have all drawn near.

A snowman winks with a carrot nose,
While icicles dangle like frozen prose.
Critters chuckle beneath the white,
In a snowy realm, it's pure delight.

Footprints lead to a snowball fight,
Each throw a burst of pure delight.
With frosty smiles, the fun unrolls,
In these winter woods, we lose control.

As the sun dips low, the laughter glows,
Even the pines wear a humor rose.
With joy and mirth, the night will fall,
In this winter land, there's fun for all.

Nimble Forms in the Dust of Time

In the dust of time, we dance and sway,
With pockets full of giggles, come what may.
The past can't catch us; we remain spry,
Nimble forms, just passing by.

Tickle the winds with a playful spin,
Eras collide where laughter begins.
A toss of dust, a glint of glee,
Moments twirl like a wild jubilee.

With echoes of chuckles from days long gone,
We kick up fun till the break of dawn.
Every turn brings a brand new rhyme,
As we skip through the dust of time.

In the loop of jokes, the clock unwinds,
Life's a series of silly finds.
Chasing mischief with every chime,
In the air of fun, we suspend time.

The Dance of Light, the Kiss of Ice

Under the glow of a silvery light,
We twirl and glide, oh what a sight!
The kiss of ice, it tickles the toes,
As laughter rises with the winter's prose.

Spinning like tops on the frozen lake,
With every slip, a new laugh we make.
The moon above seems to wink and play,
As we dance till the break of day.

Crystals shimmer in a joyous embrace,
We slide and laugh, undisguised grace.
With each silly tumble, the night feels right,
In the dance of light, oh such pure delight!

So raise a cheer for the frosty air,
For smiles abound everywhere.
In this ball of fun, the world spins bright,
Through a kiss of ice and a dance of light.

Flickering Forms in a Shattered Dream

In a shattered dream where laughter reigns,
Flickering forms dance with no chains.
They bounce and prance in the moonlit glow,
Tickled by whims only dreamers know.

A jester's cap on a playful hare,
Waving to clouds that dash through the air.
Each twirl a giggle, each leap a cheer,
In a world where nothing is ever drear.

The whispers of snowflakes join the song,
As we spin through the night, so merry and strong.
Every moment glittering with glee,
Flickering forms, just wild and free.

As dawn creeps in, the laughter fades,
But the joy remains in the winter glades.
With hearts so light, we'll find a way,
To cherish those flickers, come what may.

Serendipity in the Frosted Air

A squirrel slips and takes a dive,
In piles of snow, oh what a jive!
With a twist and a turn, it finds a treat,
Landing right on its furry feet.

Kids gather round, snowballs in hand,
Planning a strike, a snowy stand!
But mischief brews, and laughter reigns,
As one gets hit, it's all in good games.

Snowmen grinning with stick arms wide,
Wearing hats that make them glide.
But wait, what's that? A bird in a cap,
Confused, it chirps—what a silly trap!

The winter air is a canvas bright,
With giggles echoing through the night.
In frosty laughter, joy takes flight,
As snowflakes dance, wrapped in delight.

Beneath the Breath of Winter's Veil

A frosty breeze gives cheeks a glow,
As penguins waddle in a row.
Stumbling past, they trip on ice,
Making us chuckle, oh how nice!

The dog leaps high, on a quest for fun,
But in the deep snow, he's done!
Wagging his tail, he looks confused,
In winter's grip, he feels bemused.

Hot cocoa in hand, we cheer the day,
With marshmallows floating, a sweet display.
When one takes a sip and makes a face,
Spitting out snow with a funny grace!

Through winter's chill, we share a grin,
As laughter echoes, let the joy begin.
Under snowy spells, our hearts so light,
In frosted air, we find delight.

Hazy Thoughts in Crystal Time

Icicles dangling in a frozen glow,
Stalactites formed from the melting flow.
As they clank and jingle with every breeze,
Reminding us of nature's funny tease.

A cat in a beanie, prancing with flair,
Tumbles on ice, thinking it's rare!
With paws that slip and a puzzled stare,
It swipes at snowflakes, unaware of the air.

Snowflakes whisper tales of the day,
Of sledding adventures, come what may.
And we chuckle at frosty-haired friends,
With styles so wacky, laughter never ends.

In a world of white, we laugh at the chill,
With goofy glee and winter's thrill.
Through frosty fun, our dreams we weave,
In crystal times, it's hard to believe.

The Twilight's Lullaby on Ice

At twilight's edge, the world aglow,
The moon peeks out from a blanket of snow.
While skaters twirl in misfit glee,
As one takes a fall, we laugh with glee!

Snowflakes twirl like dancers on cue,
As friends collide, oh what a view!
With rosy cheeks and laughter's delight,
In frosty games, we find pure light.

A mulled wine spill on someone's shoe,
Creating puddles, a slippery brew.
They slip then slide, with arms flailing wide,
While howls of laughter echo outside.

In twilight's arms, the fun must end,
With stories told that we won't suspend.
Through winter's chill, we twinkle and grin,
As moonlit laughter wraps us within.

Lost Reflections on a White Canvas

In winter's gleam, I slipped so sly,
My boots betrayed me with a cry.
I spun around like a clumsy bear,
While snowflakes giggled without a care.

A snowman laughed with a carrot nose,
His frosty grin made me freeze and doze.
I tried to wave, but fell in style,
While snowflakes danced, I just lost my smile.

The pines stood tall, dressed in white,
They whispered secrets in the night.
I told a joke to a passing cat,
But all I got back was a frosty spat.

Oh, winter nights are quite the jest,
With frosty friends and snowball quests.
Each slip and slide, a playful cheer,
While snowflakes chuckled, come hear, come near!

A Dance of Frost and Night

Beneath the stars, I took a chance,
In fluffy boots, I tried to dance.
With every twirl, I lost my grip,
And belly-flopped on a snowdrift dip.

The owls hooted, what a sight,
As I flopped around in pure delight.
A snowflake landed on my nose,
I laughed so hard, off my balance I froze.

With twinkling lights and moonbeams bright,
Lost in laughter, a silly plight.
The trees were clapping, or so I thought,
But really, they just knew I had fought.

Oh, winter evenings steal the show,
With giggles warm amidst the snow.
Each icy step, a slip or fall,
In the dance of winter, I had a ball!

Eclipsed Forms in the Silent Chill

In a snowy field, I saw a wight,
With glowing eyes in the frosty night.
I waved hello with a frozen hand,
But it was just my own boot in the sand.

The snowflakes whispered, secrets spun,
I quipped a joke, but it was all in fun.
A hapless snowball flew past my ear,
It turned to ice and disappeared, oh dear!

An igloo stood with a comical tilt,
Inside, my jokes were met with guilt.
The penguins chuckled from afar,
As I sculpted a snowman that looked bizarre.

With frozen breath, I shared a grin,
While snowmen danced, trying to win.
Each flurry of fun, a chilly prank,
In winter's glow, my laughter sank!

The Stillness Between Heartbeats on Ice

On a frozen pond, I took my glide,
But tripped on my skates and fell with pride.
The ice cracked jokes, or was that me?
As I flopped around like a lost bumblebee.

A twirling spin turned awkwardly bright,
As I waved to folks with all my might.
But gravity struck, and down I went,
A plop in the snow, my ego bent!

Laughter rang through the chilly air,
A snowball squad joined my frosty despair.
They targeted me with a crafty aim,
But I dodged and tripped – oh, what a game!

With each cold breath and giggly cheer,
I found my rhythm, winter's sincere.
For in this stillness, oh what glee,
As ice and laughter set my heart free!

Pale Forms in the Glistening Stillness

In the quiet, something stirs,
A snowman wears a carrot nose,
But look real close, oh what a sight,
It's just my dog in winter's pose.

A snowflake lands upon my cheek,
I giggle; they tickle with glee,
Then watch my hat go tumbling down,
The only thing still, not me!

My raccoon friend with paws outstretched,
Tried to steal my mittens fine,
Now he's stuck in a snowdrift deep,
I can't stop laughing, he's divine!

The cold air's filled with laughter bright,
Each slip and fall brings joy anew,
As we frolic, slip, and slide,
This winter's playground just for two!

The Hush of Illusion on a Frozen Lake.

Upon the ice, we dance around,
A troupe of penguins, we pretend,
But one falls flat, the others laugh,
A sea of giggles doesn't end.

With every glide, we twist and turn,
Hoping to unleash our best moves,
But someone finds a frosty spot,
And suddenly, the ice approves!

As ducks above quack out a tune,
We swirl and twirl, in pure delight,
While Charlie curls up, takes a nap,
Dreaming of using wings in flight.

So here we are: a frozen crew,
With moments caught, and laughter shared,
In every slip, a twist of fate,
A winter ballet, unprepared!

Winter's Whispering Veils

The snowflakes giggle as they land,
Covering our boots with fluff,
But wait! My foot's stuck in a mound,
I think I've found the fluffiest stuff!

With every toss of flaky white,
A pillow fight might just ensue,
But someone slips, instead of aims,
And from the pile, we all go 'woo!'

Sledding down the hills so steep,
Zooming fast, a comedic race,
But as we crash into a tree,
Our laughter fills the frosty space.

So let's rejoice, in snowy fun,
And dance like snowflakes in the breeze,
For winter's charm is never clear,
Unless you fall beforehand, wheeze!

Frosted Echoes Beneath Twilight

As twilight creeps on snowy slopes,
A snowball's launched, straight at my nose,
With laughter echoing in the night,
A face full of frost, oh how it glows!

The trees are draped in sparkling white,
Like they've donned gowns for a ball,
Yet when I trip, and down I go,
I'm quite the jester with my fall.

My friends and I, so full of cheer,
Create a snow angel brigade,
But oh! The wings are less than grand,
More like a pancake, I was laid!

With stars above and hearts so light,
We race beneath the moon's soft hue,
In frosted echoes, laughter rings,
Our winter tales forever true!

Shadowed Hints of Yesteryear

In a park where squirrels play,
A scarf's lost, bright and gay.
A snowball flies, with laughter loud,
We duck and dodge, lost in the crowd.

A snowman stands, a frosty foe,
With a carrot nose, stealing the show.
He grins wide, his buttons askew,
Looks just like me, if only I knew!

The chilly air, a playful tease,
Chasing pals like winter's breeze.
We stumble and slide, all in a row,
And trip over footprints, oh what a show!

As we build our frosted pride,
With each big scoop, we can't abide,
Giggling fits while snowflakes fall,
We find our joy within the squall.

Fragments of Wonder in the Snow

Wonders wrapped in white delight,
As snowflakes dance in the moonlight.
A rabbit hops, a puff of fluff,
We can't help but giggle – enough's enough!

Tiny hats of snowy cream,
On every head, they twist and gleam.
With each plop, we make our claims,
Of who can build the tall snow dames!

Beneath the trees, a treasure lies,
An igloo made of laughing cries.
We stumble in, just two by two,
The snowman's jealous – he wants in too!

As evening falls, we sip hot drinks,
And share our dreams as the paper shrinks.
With eyes alight, we seek the glow,
In friendships warm, as cold winds blow.

Quiet Currents in the Winter Breeze

A gust whirls in the chilly air,
Whispering secrets, unaware.
We race along, with giggles bright,
And chase our breaths, in soft moonlight.

With every step, we hear a crunch,
In boots that squish, we laugh and munch.
The trees are bare, but spirits high,
Winter's grin, as we pass by.

A mitten lost, a sock adrift,
As snowflakes fall, our laughter lifts.
We gather all the gooey white,
Creating chaos, pure delight!

Beneath the stars, we weave our tales,
Of frosty dreams and winter gales.
With every jig, the world feels right,
In joyful dance, we embrace the night.

The Enigma of Soft White Layers

Layers thick, a puzzling sight,
Blankets spread in the soft moonlight.
A snowball fight, let the games commence,
Just watch your aim, or face consequence!

Laughing faces, cheeks aglow,
A slippery path, oh no, oh no!
With every slip, our laughter grows,
Like winter's magic, see how it flows!

Pirates of fluff, we are stout,
A quest for treasure, without a doubt!
With maps of snow and hearts that sing,
We've found the joy that winters bring!

As twilight fades, we gather near,
With stories spun, and voices clear.
In every flake lies a funny tale,
Of winter's charm in a snowy veil.

Unraveled Designs on the Purest Ground

A snowman stands with a lopsided hat,
His carrot nose adds to the chat.
"Is it fashion?" he seems to say,
"Or did my builder run away?"

The frostbit toes of winter gloat,
As penguins waddle in a loud coat.
But who, I ask, would steal my drink?
The ice cube laughs, I pause to think!

The chilly breeze whispers a jest,
As snowflakes giggle, it's all a fest.
With snowballs flying left and right,
It's comedy central; what a sight!

So here we dance, with frosty grace,
In swirling snow, this happy place.
A winter wonder, laughing bright,
In nature's quilt of white delight.

Silent Watchers in a Winter's Tale

The trees all wear a coat of white,
With branches bent, a clumsy sight.
A squirrel slips, what a loud thud!
While snowflakes giggle, "What's this mud?"

The owls hoot, with puzzled frowns,
As frostbit critters shuffle 'round.
I swear I saw a moose in boots,
Accompanied by dancing toots!

A frozen lake, where ducks now skate,
They trade old tales of winter's fate.
While oversized mittens float on by,
A snowball fight breaks out nearby!

So bundle up for the frosty flake,
With frosty friends, we laugh and shake.
In silent watch, let joy prevail,
As laughter echoes through this tale.

Forgotten Dreams in the Deep Freeze

The winter night brings frosty dreams,
Where icicles dance and starlight beams.
Yet in the chill, a sock brigade,
Is lost from dryers, unreplayed!

A snowball's launched, a direct hit,
The target fumbles, takes a split!
"Is this a game or just a mess?"
"We'll call it both! Now, who'll confess?"

A snowman's got a carrot plight,
His nose is gone; it's quite a fright!
The gnome knocks twice, starts monologuing,
While rabbits munch with no jogging!

In twilight hues, we find our cheer,
As winter spins its tale sincere.
Forgotten dreams in laughter's freeze,
In whimsy's grip, we feel at ease.

An Ode to Frost-touched Figures

Oh, frosty friends with twinkling eyes,
With scarves askew, in joyful guise.
You trip and slip on this icy track,
With silly faces, not looking back!

A winter blizzard swirls about,
As cheerful gnomes begin to shout.
"Grab your sled, let's race on down!"
But bumping snowmen makes us frown!

The flurries spin, and laughter roars,
As penguins slide through open doors.
A frozen frog joins in the fun,
While icicles bask in winter sun!

So here's to all the frosty haze,
To winter's craft and silly ways.
In chill and glee, our hearts align,
With frost-touched figures, life's divine!

Secrets Whispered by the Frozen Bleak

A snowman grinned beneath the trees,
His carrot nose caught quite the breeze.
He whispered jokes to frozen birds,
In giggles muffled, they sang their words.

A snowflake falls, a daring tease,
It splats on a puppy, oh how it flees!
The dog jumps back, a comet in fright,
As children laugh at the comical sight.

Icicles dangle like pointy fangs,
A careful step, and their humor hangs.
They giggle as they melt in the sun,
Winter's trick is a slippery run!

The frost-bitten grass, all coated in white,
Lies beneath the snow, a pure delight.
When spring comes around with a mischievous grin,
We'll watch as flowers and laughter begin!

Forgotten Whispers in the Winter's Chill

A penguin wobbles, not quite a slide,
On frosty ground, he tumbles wide.
He shakes his flippers, a dance so absurd,
While snowflakes giggle, they whisper their word.

Sleds race wildly, kids hit a bump,
Flying through air, a glorious jump!
Lands with a thud in snowbanks so deep,
Creating a snow angel that's half asleep.

The carrot tops poke out from the ground,
Where bunnies thrill at the wintery sound.
They munch and crunch on a secret stash,
While squirrels chuckle, ready to splash.

The chilly breeze knows all of their tales,
Of frosty antics and slippery trails.
With laughter hanging, the cold holds tight,
In frozen whispers, the world feels light!

Lonesome Figures Beneath the Moon's Gaze

A snowshoe hare hops, doing the twist,
Under moonlight's glow, hard to resist.
With each little leap, he makes a joke,
And wraps the night in a soft white cloak.

The stars twinkle slyly, a wink and a grin,
While bears snooze in caves, they dream of din.
A midnight feast of honey and pie,
Though winter's feast, they lazily sigh.

An owl hoots softly, "The party's begun!"
With snowy robes and a laugh, he runs.
He does a small jig, atop icy logs,
With winter's light showing off the fogs.

Yet still there lingers, a chilly comrade,
With frozen toes in an icy parade.
But laughter rises in the cool night air,
As creatures gather, all unaware!

The Veil of Ice and Flickering Light

A firefly flicks in the nighttime chill,
Twirling around with a luminous thrill.
It dances on snow, a peculiar sight,
Foolishly daring the frosty bite.

A polar bear coughs, he sneezes a flare,
Sending snowflakes high, into the air.
The snow faces giggle, all sneezed out in cheer,
As winter whispers, "Hey, bring on the beer!"

A raccoon pops up from beneath a mound,
With twinkling eyes, he jumps all around.
In a world of ice, he's a merry prank,
Playing with shadows, oh how he clanks!

As the moon grins, all things become bright,
With snowball fights in the cusp of night.
The cold cannot freeze all the joyous plays,
In a veil of ice, the laughter stays!

Shadows of Memory in White Silence

A snowman grins, his carrot nose,
Whispers of winter, anything goes.
The dog walks sideways, trying to prance,
In fluffy white boots, he can't help but glance.

The children giggle, sleds in a pile,
Launching like rockets, it's quite a while.
Hot cocoa smiles, marshmallows afloat,
Warming those fingers, while snowmen gloat.

A snowball fight erupts with loud cheers,
And a cat, in horror, just stares through tears.
The snowflakes dance, like tiny confetti,
While grandpa mutters, "This is so petty!"

In white-thick laughter, they'll find a way,
To keep the chill off—hip hip hooray!
With snowflakes falling, all frosty and bright,
Winter's a joke, wrapped up in delight.

Frost-kissed Reveries

A penguin waddles, with style so grand,
In a frozen disco, he starts a band.
The snowflakes twirl like they're in a spree,
While squirrels go wild with their acorn tea.

With boots made of rubber, we stomp in the snow,
The boots squish loud—listen to them go!
A snow angel flops, then giggles, oh dear,
The art of the flurry, let's give it a cheer!

Snow forts arise like castles of white,
With marshmallow guards to protect from the night.
The blizzard laughs, it slips on a hat,
And giggles at all the silly chit-chat.

Round in the cold, we tumble and slide,
Through valleys of laughter, winter's our guide.
With a snow-covered world, all so absurd,
There's nothing like joy without a word!

Strange Shapes in the Quiet Drift

An elephant's trunk, so oddly placed,
A low-flying reindeer, quite out of space.
The snow glints laughter, in weird disguise,
As snowflakes tumble, in topsy surprise.

With snowmen sprouting, all goofy and bright,
One tips his hat, and gets quite a fright.
The igloo's a mansion, complete with a door,
Where penguins sip drinks on a frosty floor.

A tickled tree twists in the chilly breeze,
Who knew dumb old pines could dance with such ease?
An upside-down sled sits stuck on a hill,
Makes winter quite mad, yet somehow still chill.

So come join the fun, this melted brigade,
Where laughter and winter are perfectly made.
Through tangled snowdrifts, come find us, you'll see,
In a world of snow shapes, it's funny as can be!

Mirage Beneath the Blinding White

A snowflake whispers, "See my grand show!"
While a squirrel attempts to ski in the snow.
Feet in the air, he declares, "I'm a star!"
But lands on his belly, a hilarious czar.

With snowball explosions, laughter erupts,
As kids in the turmoil get always disrupted.
Frozen surprises, like snowmen on ice,
Will two-headed gnomes be here? Oh, how nice!

Hot chocolate with sprinkles, a sweet frosty treat,
Turned into a slick sled, slipping off feet.
While their cheeks turn pink in the shimmer and glow,
Wintertime antics steal every show.

Beneath all the layers, we giggle and play,
While winter throws pranks, joy leads the way.
The mirage of laughter, beneath the cold sky,
In a world full of nonsense, oh how we fly!

Milton Keynes UK
Ingram Content Group UK Ltd.
UKHW020741221124
451186UK00024B/151